HAL LEONARD STUDENT PIANO LIBRARY

Classical Themes

Favorite orchestral works arranged for piano solo
by Fred Kern, Phillip Keveren, and Mona Rejino

Text Author
Barbara Kreader

Editor
Margaret Otwell

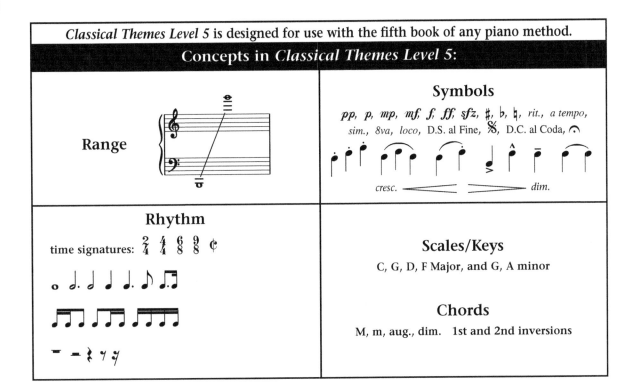

Classical Themes Level 5 is designed for use with the fifth book of any piano method.

Concepts in *Classical Themes Level 5*:

Range

Symbols

pp, p, mp, mf, f, ff, sfz, ♯, ♭, ♮, *rit., a tempo, sim., 8va, loco,* D.S. al Fine, 𝄋, D.C. al Coda, 𝄐

cresc. ——————— *dim.*

Rhythm

time signatures: 2/4 4/4 6/8 9/8 ¢

Scales/Keys

C, G, D, F Major, and G, A minor

Chords

M, m, aug., dim.   1st and 2nd inversions

To access audio visit:
www.halleonard.com/mylibrary

Enter Code
5372-2631-5283-9553

ISBN 978-1-4950-4698-8

HAL•LEONARD® CORPORATION

7777 W. BLUEMOUND RD. P.O. BOX 13819 MILWAUKEE, WI 53213

In Australia Contact:
Hal Leonard Australia Pty. Ltd.
4 Lentara Court
Cheltenham, Victoria, 3192 Australia
Email: ausadmin@halleonard.com.au

Visit Hal Leonard Online at
www.halleonard.com

Table of Contents

About the Compositions

Love Theme from the ballet ROMEO AND JULIET.. 7
Pyotr Il'yich Tchaikovsky (1840-1893)

Beginning in 1869, the composer Balakirev helped his Russian countryman Pyotr Il'yich Tchaikovsky work out his ideas for the ballet, *Romeo and Juliet.* The content of the music is highly romantic and imaginative, chronicling the course of Shakespeare's heart-rending play. The music alternately depicts, in vividly contrasting themes, the violent hostility between the Capulet and Montague families and the two lovers' passionate journey into each other's hearts and arms. The ballet's final scene, a funeral march for Romeo and Juliet, is based on the famous *Love Theme* that characterizes their growing love throughout the ballet.

Also Sprach Zarathustra Opening Theme...10
Richard Strauss (1864-1949)

The German composer Richard Strauss wrote progressive music based on literary or philosophical concepts. While the topics of his works were highly intellectual, Strauss often used realistic imagery in his music, such as the sound of sheep in his symphonic poem *Don Juan.* He also entertained such early twentieth-century beliefs as the possibility for the individual to change the world and control his destiny. Despite his forward-thinking philosophies, Strauss, for the most part, chose to write his works in traditional classical forms. The symphonic poems *Don Juan* and *Macbeth* use the sonata form, and *Don Quixote* is a set of extended variations. Strauss' symphonic poem, *Also Sprach Zarathustra,* is based on a book of the same name by the German philosopher Frederich Nietzsche. Strauss fashioned this work on the philosophical ideas found in the book's prologue and eighty of its subsequent chapters.

Symphony No. 40 First Movement Theme 12
Wolfgang Amadeus Mozart (1756-1791)

The Viennese composer Wolfgang Amadeus Mozart wrote over 50 symphonies. During the Classic period, the symphony usually served as a prelude to music of greater significance. As a form, it had not gained the prominence that Beethoven later bestowed on it. Only two of Mozart's symphonies, and very few of his other works, use the key of G minor, a key he turns to for those heart-rending outpourings of sorrow and despair that we find in some of his opera scenes. This symphony was completed in 1788. Its harmonic boldness, contrapuntal mastery, adventurous harmonies, and instrumental color show Mozart at the top of his form.

Jesu, Joy of Man's Desiring from CANTATA NO. 147 16
Johann Sebastian Bach (1685-1750)

In his own day, the German composer Johann Sebastian Bach was considered old-fashioned. He still used heavy ornamentation, such as trills and mordents, and his music remained decidedly polyphonic (many voices playing at once) at a time when younger composers were giving melody more emphasis. However, in many of his works, Bach masterfully combines the abstract style and complex musical textures of Baroque music with a sublime spiritual and expressive depth — the equal of which is rarely found in other composers' works of the same period. *Jesu, Joy of Man's Desiring* does display a clear, extended melody, even though the setting contains several independant voices. It remains one of Bach's most popular works.

Air On The G String from the ORCHESTRAL SUITE NO. 3
Johann Sebastian Bach (1685-1750)

Johann Sebastian Bach was the most important member of a German family of musicians renowned from the 16th to the 19th century. A huge number of fiddlers, town musicians, organists, *Kantors*, court musicians, and *Kappelmeisters* shared the name "Bach." J.S. Bach wrote most of his music for church events, writing amazing numbers of motets, oratorios, chorales, sacred songs, and keyboard music for organ and harpsichord. Although he was a noted organ virtuoso, Bach was not well-known as a composer during his lifetime. Fewer than a dozen of his compositions were printed while he lived. Only when Felix Mendelssohn produced a revival performance of Bach's great choral work, the *St. Matthew Passion*, in 1829, did Bach's music begin to receive the reverence it commands today.

Sicilienne
Gabriel Fauré (1845-1924)

The French composer Gabriel Fauré studied with Saint-Saëns, who helped launch his composing career in the 1870s. Fauré wrote much religious music, including his famous *Requiem,* written after his mother's death. Yet, his heart was not in such music, nor in organ playing, choir conducting, or private teaching – all of which he abandoned after he became Director of the Paris Conservatoire in 1905. Fauré believed the purpose of art and music was to *"...elevate mankind as far as possible above everyday existence."* His later works, such as the *Second Piano Quartet* (1919-1921) and the *Piano Trio* (1922-1923) are forceful and powerful works. Fauré holds together opposing elements such as anguish and serenity using a single, unique style. He was almost alone, among French composers of his time, in not coming under the spell of Richard Wagner. Fauré composed the instrumental gem, *Sicilienne,* for cello and piano in 1893.

William Tell Theme from the Overture
Gioacchino Rossini (1792-1868)

The Italian composer Gioacchino Rossini's opera *William Tell* is rarely heard today, yet its famous overture lives on. The story takes place during an Austrian occupation of Switzerland. Gessler, a tyrannical Austrian ruler, enters William Tell's village and tries to make the Swiss give allegiance to his hat on a pole. William Tell refuses, so Gessler orders him to shoot an apple from his son's head with his crossbow. The shot succeeds, but Tell informs Gessler that had the first arrow missed its mark, the second would have been aimed at Gessler. Tell is arrested. After many battles and the burning down of Tell's house, the Swiss prevail and Tell goes free. The final, and most famous section of the overture consists of a trumpet call and a lively, fast-tempo theme representing the Swiss call to arms.

Hungarian Dance No. 5
Johannes Brahms (1833-1887)

The German composer Johannes Brahms came from a poor, but musical, family. His father played the bass in the theatre and in the Hamburg Philharmonic orchestra. A noted town musician, Edward Marxson, recognizing Brahms' talent, gave him free piano lessons. This training proved practical, for Brahms, from an early age, was able to eke out a modest, if unsavory, living by playing the piano in Hamburg's rough seaport taverns. Brahms composed the *Hungarian Dances* for piano duet during the years 1852-1869. During this time, he had the opportunity to meet Franz Liszt in Weimar and to become fast friends with Robert and Clara Schumann. These contacts, plus the successful premier of his *German Requiem,* led to his life-long relationship with the publisher Simrock, gaining Brahms the financial stability that had eluded him in his younger years.

The Italian violinist and composer Antonio Vivaldi did much to advance and develop both violin playing and the concerto form. He wrote over 500 concertos, 350 of which were for one solo instrument and strings, over 230 of them for violin. His work *The Four Seasons* remains popular partly because of its breathtaking solo-violin parts. A virtuoso violinist himself, Vivaldi's performances often produced the audience awe evident in this review*: "Vivaldi performed a solo accompaniment [to an aria] admirably, and at the end he improvised a fantasy which quite confounded me, for such playing has never before been equaled; he played his fingers but a hair's breadth from the bridge, so that there was hardly room for the bow. He played thus on all four strings, with imitations and at unbelievable speed."*

The French composer Camille Saint-Saëns' suite, *Carnival Of The Animals* (1866) mimics the sounds and movements of several animals: swans, elephants, lions – even pianists! Saint-Saëns originally wrote this suite for a small chamber ensemble that included two pianos, and later arranged it for a large-scale orchestra. He publicly disavowed its enormous popularity, claiming he had only written the work as a moment's diversion. The poet Ogden Nash later wrote humorous poetry for each piece. Today, concert performances of *Carnival Of The Animals* often include a narrator, who reads Nash's witty, poetic animal characterizations before the musical depiction of each one.

Love Theme
from the ballet ROMEO AND JULIET

Pyotr Il'yich Tchaikovsky (1840 – 1893)
Russia
originally for orchestra
Arranged by Phillip Keveren

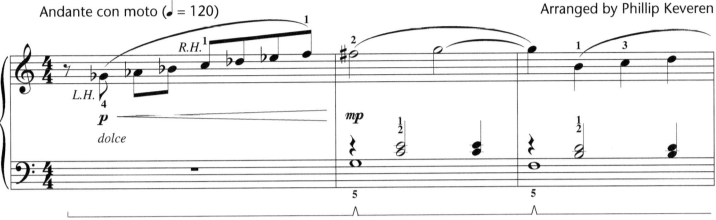

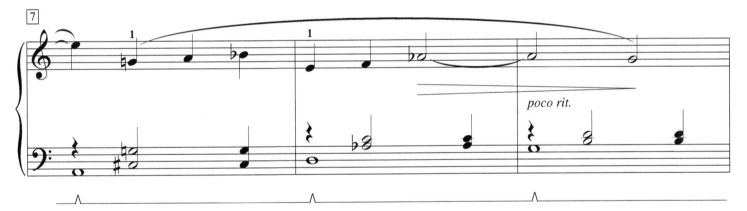

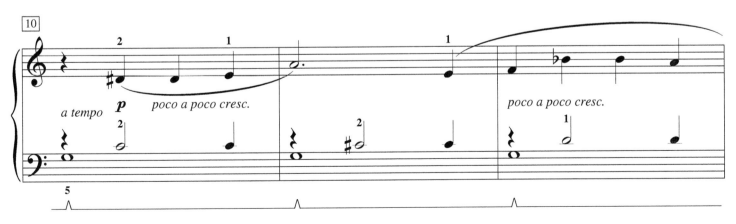

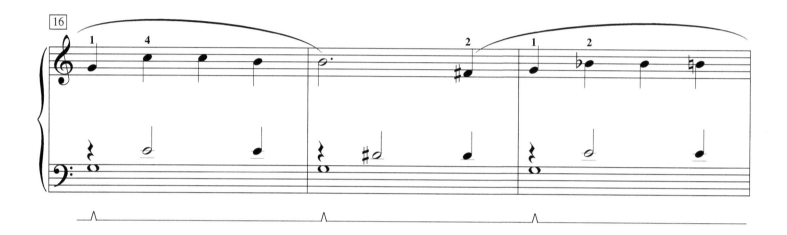

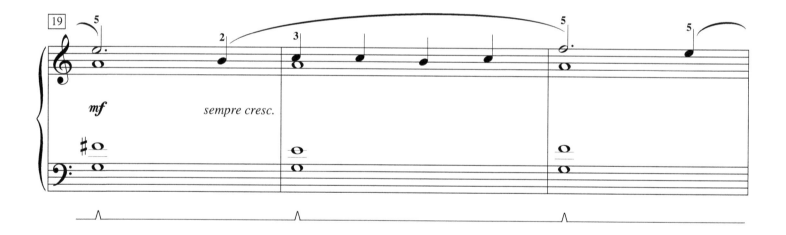

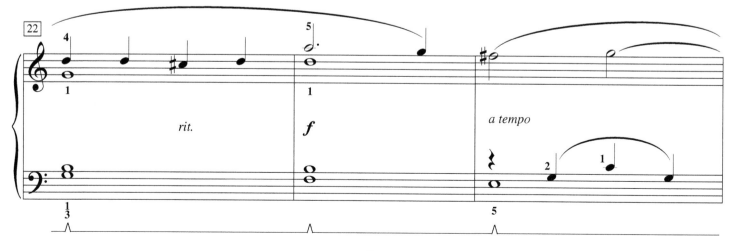

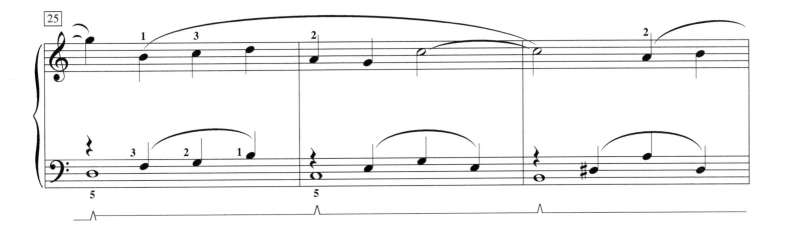

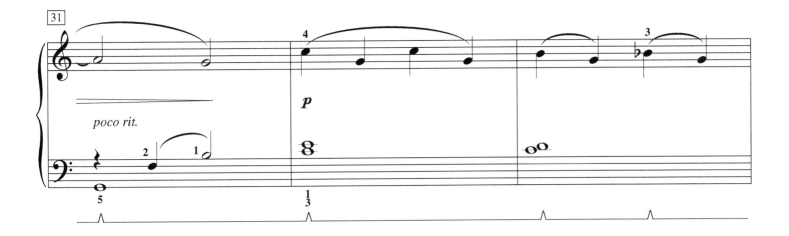

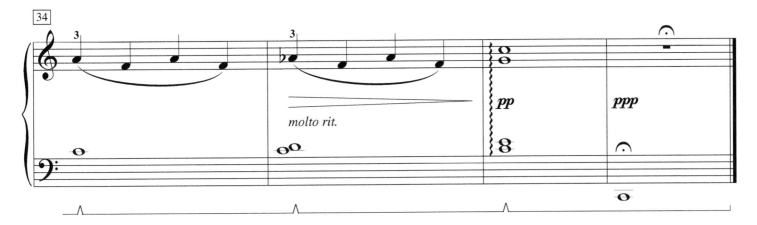

Also Sprach Zarathustra

Opening Theme

Richard Strauss (1864 – 1949)
Germany
originally for orchestra
Arranged by Phillip Keveren

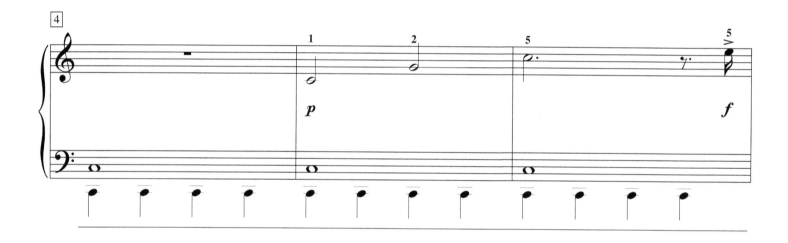

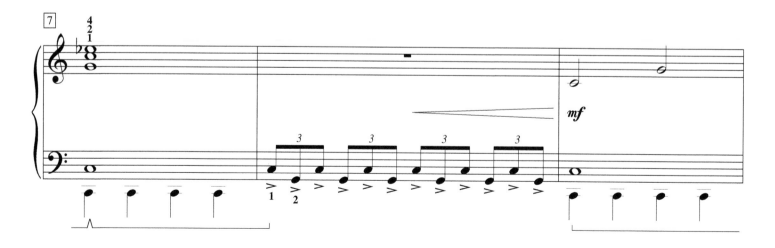

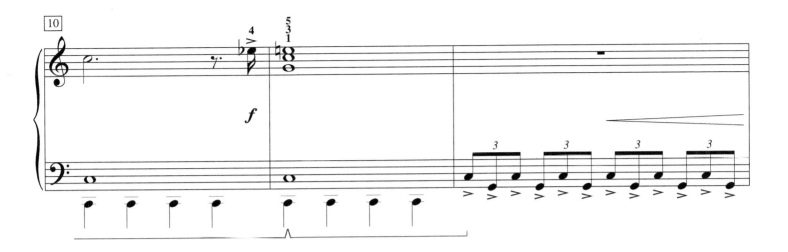

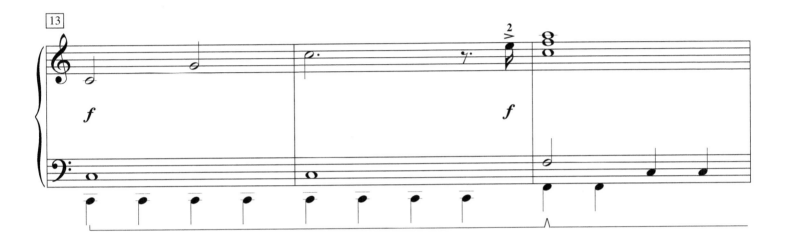

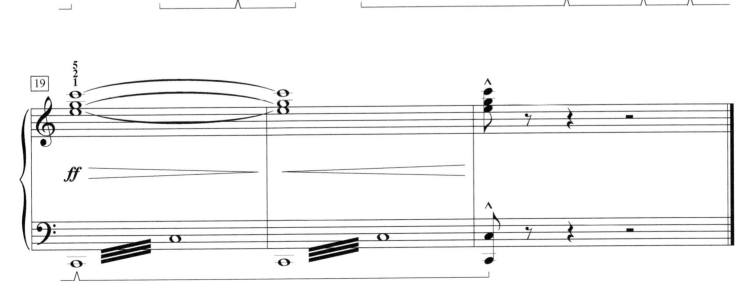

Symphony No. 40

First Movement Theme

Wolfgang Amadeus Mozart (1756 – 1791)
Austria
originally for orchestra
Arranged by Phillip Keveren

Allegro molto (♩ = 100)

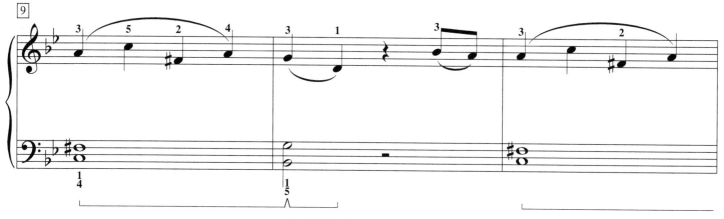

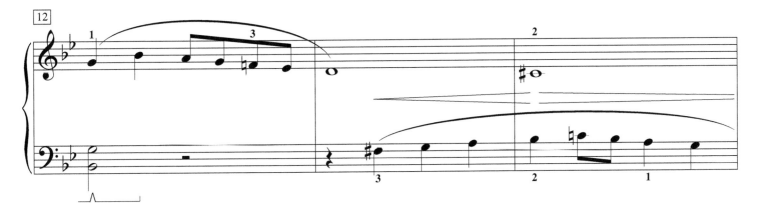

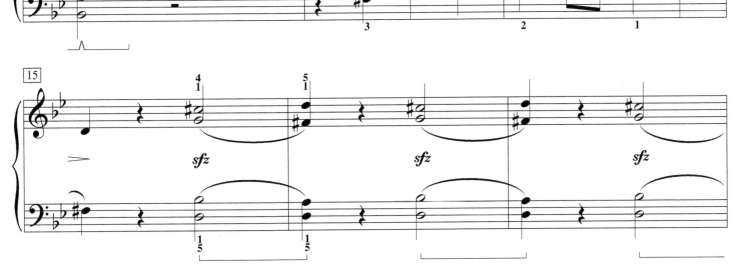

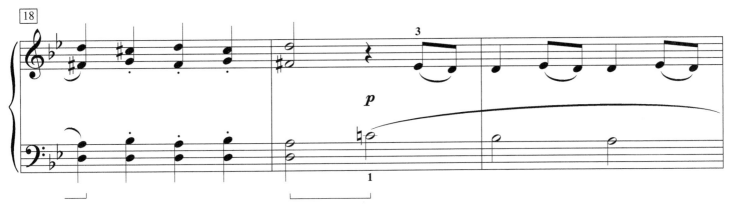

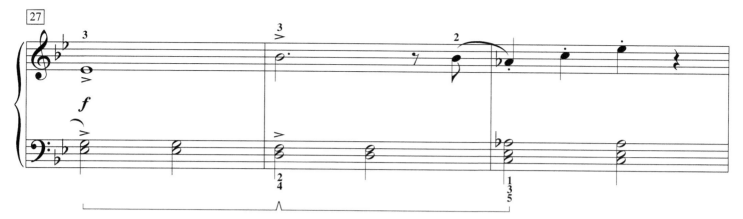

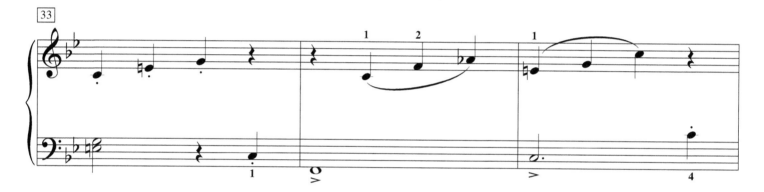

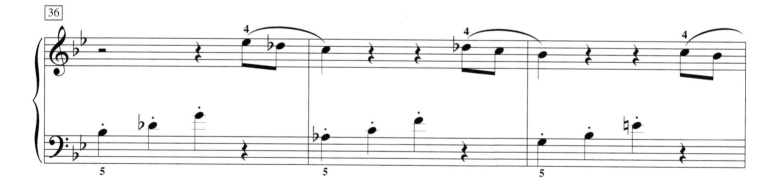

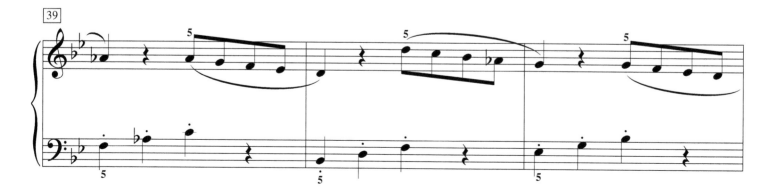

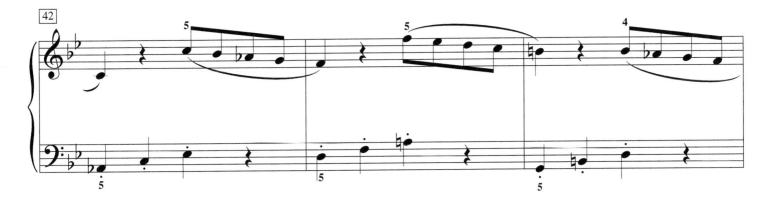

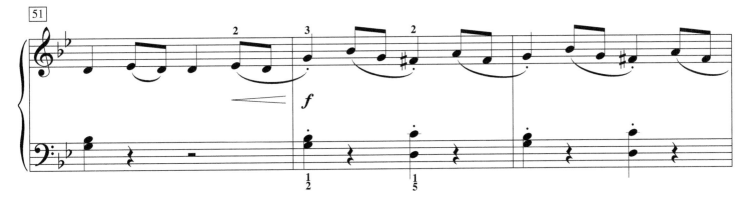

15

Jesu, Joy Of Man's Desiring

from CANTATA NO. 147

Johann Sebastian Bach (1685 – 1750)
Germany
originally for chorus and orchestra
Arranged by Fred Kern

Moderato (♩. = 60)

To Coda ⊕

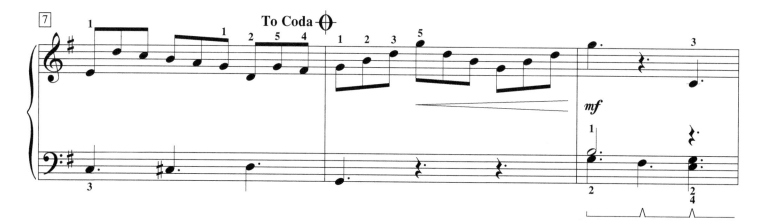

CODA

Air On The G String
from the ORCHESTRAL SUITE NO. 3

Johann Sebastian Bach (1685 – 1750)
Germany
originally for orchestra
Arranged by Fred Kern

Adagio (♩ = 69)

(Play L.H. detached throughout.)

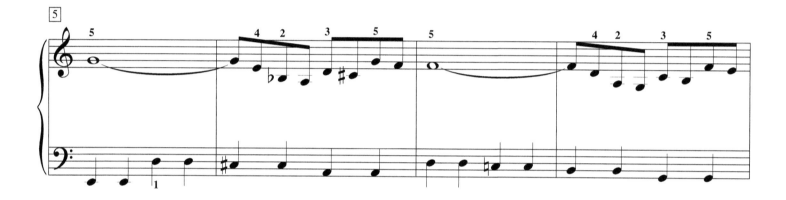

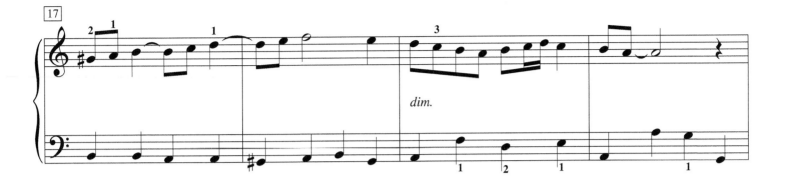

Sicilienne

Gabriel Fauré (1845 – 1924)
France
originally for cello and piano
Arranged by Phillip Keveren

Andantino (♩. = 48)

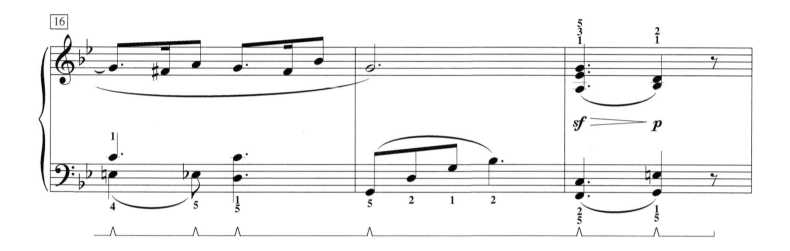

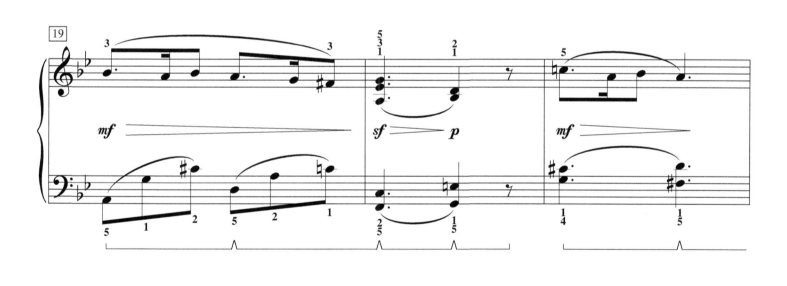

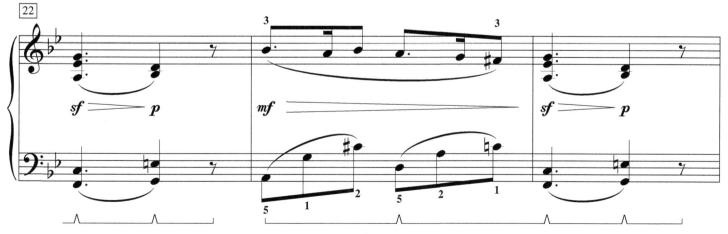

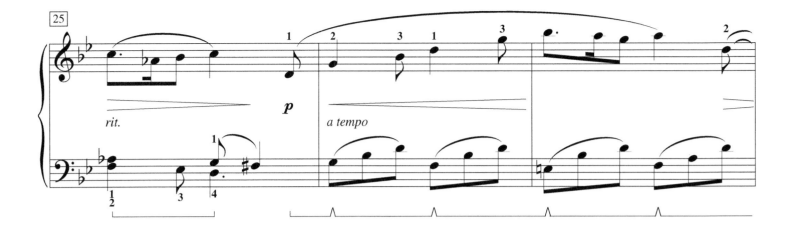

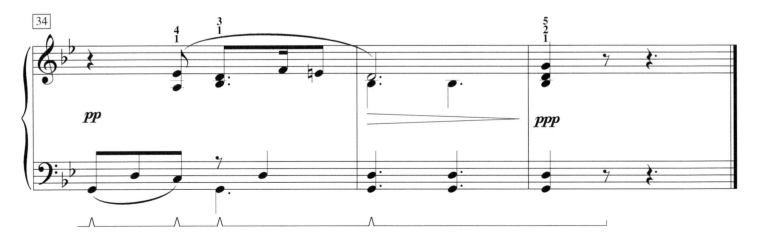

William Tell
Theme from the Overture

Gioacchino Rossini (1792 – 1868)
Italy
originally for orchestra
Arranged by Mona Rejino

Allegro vivace (♩ = 104)

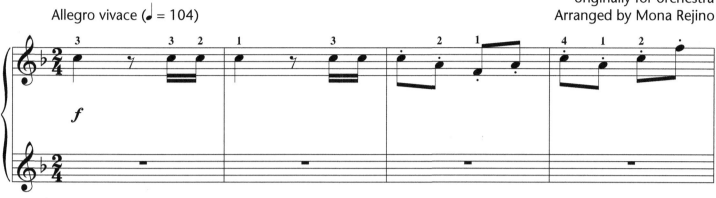

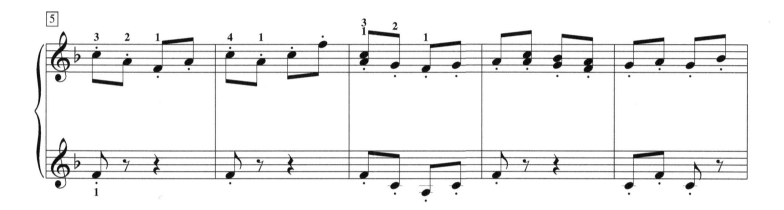

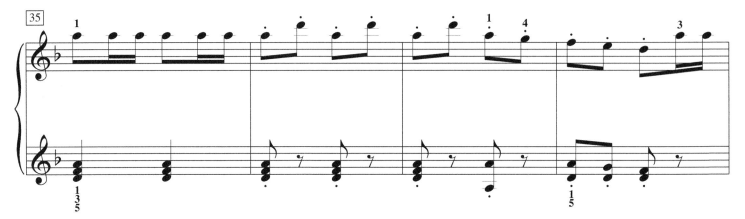

24

D.S. al Fine

Hungarian Dance No. 5

Johannes Brahms (1833 – 1897)
Germany
originally for piano duet; later arranged for orchestra
Arranged by Mona Rejino

Allegro (♩ = 100)

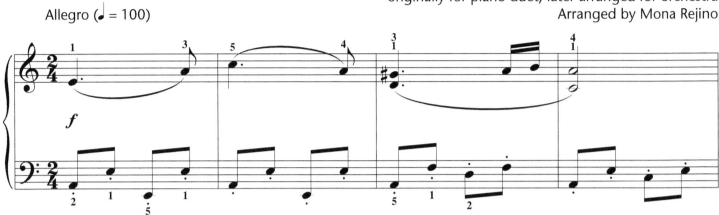

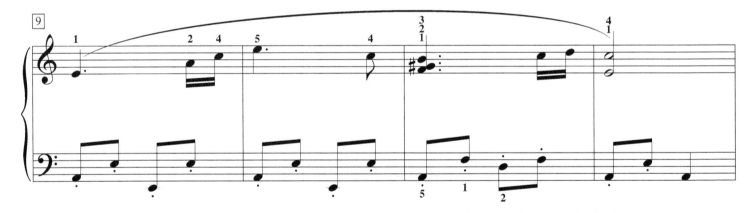

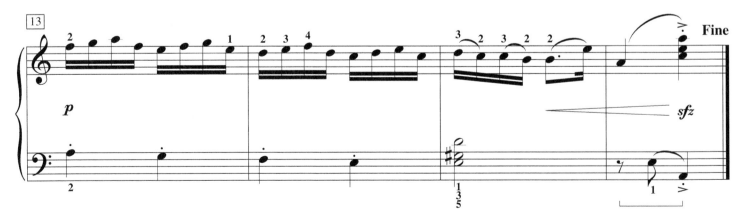

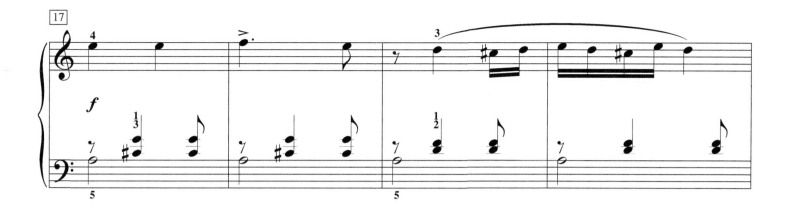

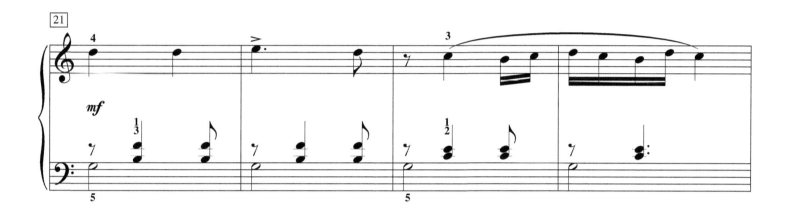

D.C. al Fine

Spring

from THE FOUR SEASONS

Antonio Vivaldi (1678 – 1741)
Italy
originally for violin and orchestra
Arranged by Mona Rejino

Allegro (♩ = 96)

Carnival Of The Animals

Finale

Camille Saint-Saëns (1835 – 1921)
France
originally for chamber ensemble
Arranged by Fred Kern

Molto Allegro (♩ = 144)

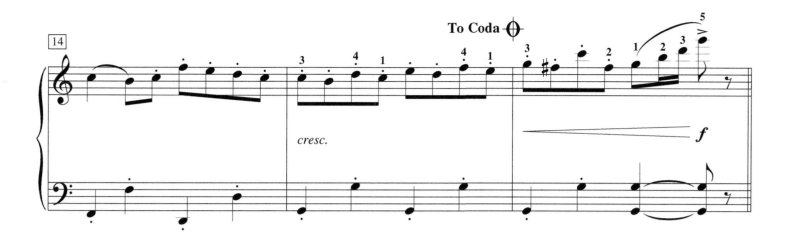

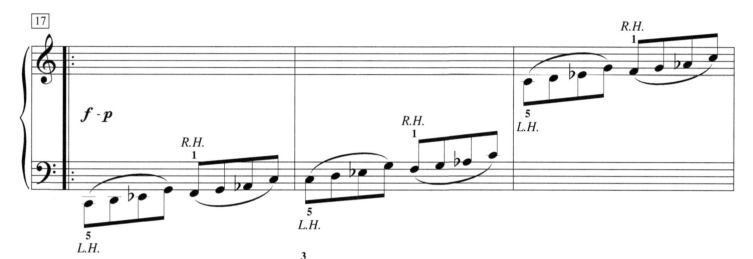

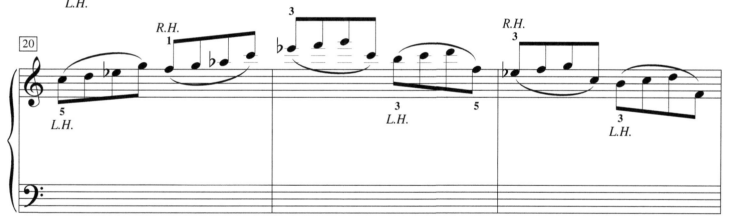

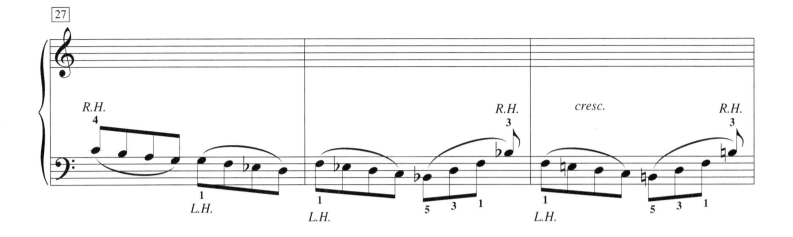

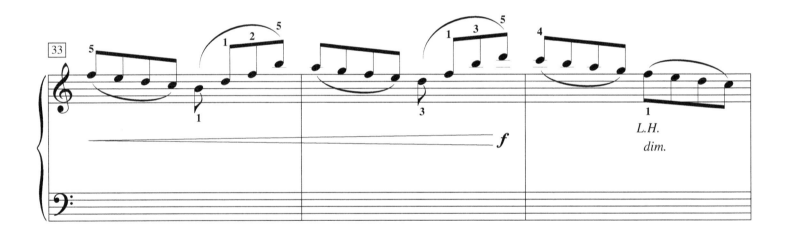

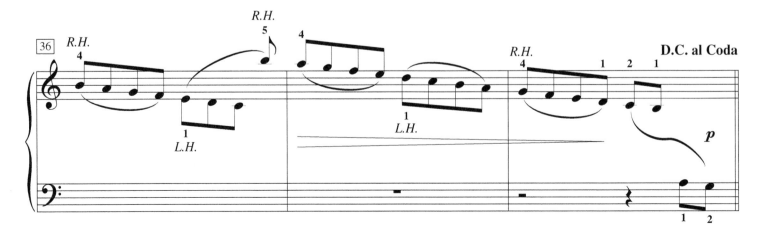

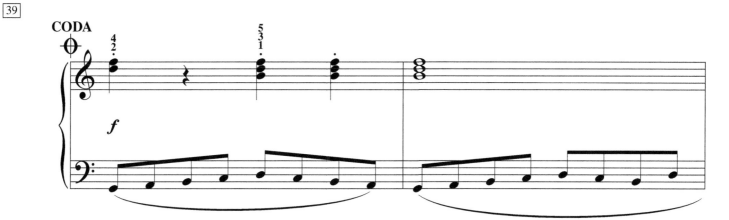

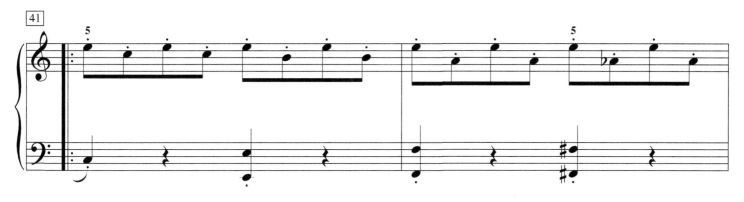

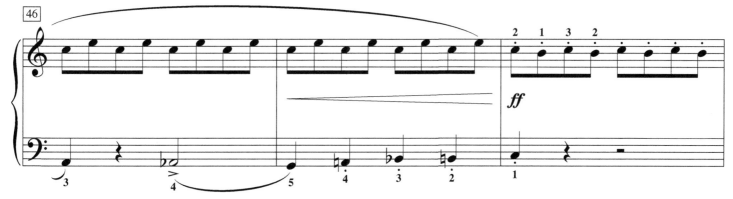

Music History Timeline

THE MIDDLE AGES

400 AD	600	800	1000	1200	1400

MUSIC

During the Middle Ages (also called the *Medieval Period*), the Roman Catholic church was the most powerful influence in European life. The church's music was a collection of ancient melodies called *plainsong* or *chant*, sung in unison (single line) with Latin words. The chants were organized in about 600 AD by Pope Gregory, and these official versions are known as *Gregorian chant*. Later, simple harmonies were added, and eventually the harmony parts became independent melodies sung with the main tune. This is called *polyphony*. Church music was written down using *neumes*, or square notes.

Outside the churches, traveling entertainers called *troubadours* or *minstrels* would sing songs about life and love in the language of the common people. This music was more lively and would often be accompanied by a drum, a wooden flute or an early form of the guitar called a *lute*.

- Plainsong
- Gregorian Chant
- Harmony
- Polyphony
- Troubadours

400 AD	600	800	1000	1200	1400

ART & LITERATURE

- Dante, author
  (The Divine Comedy)
- Romanesque architecture
- Chaucer, author
  (Canterbury Tales)
- Gothic architecture
- Donatello, artist *(David)*

400 AD	600	800	1000	1200	1400

WORLD EVENTS

- Fall of Roman Empire *(476 AD)*
- Charlemagne, Holy Roman Emperor
- First Crusade begins *(1096)*
- The Black Death *(bubonic plague)*
- Rise of European universities
- Muhammad, prophet of Islam faith
- The Magna Carta *(1215)*
- Hindu-Arabic numbers developed
- Gunpowder, compass, paper invented *(China)*
- Genghis Kahn rules Asia
- Marco Polo travels to China
- Mayan civilization
- Incan and Aztec civilizations

THE RENAISSANCE

1450	1500	1550	1600

MUSIC

The era from about 1450–1600 was called the *Renaissance* ("rebirth") because people wanted to recreate the artistic and scientific glories of ancient Greece and Rome. It was also a time of discovery. The new printing press brought music to the homes of the growing middle class. European society became more *secular*, or non-religious, and concerts were featured in the halls of the nobility. An entertaining form of secular songs was the *madrigal*, sung by 4 or 5 voices at many special occasions. Instrumental music became popular, as new string, brass and woodwind instruments were developed.

A form of church music was the *motet*, with 3 or 4 independent vocal parts. In the new Protestant churches, the entire congregation sang *chorales*: simple melodies in even rhythms like the hymns we hear today. Important Renaissance composers were Josquin des Pres, Palestrina, Gabrielli, Monteverdi, William Byrd and Thomas Tallis.

• Protestant church music

• First printed music   • Madrigals

1450	1500	1550	1600

ART & LITERATURE

• Leonardo da Vinci, scientist/artist
(*Mona Lisa, The Last Supper*)

• Michelangelo, artist
(*Sistine Chapel, David*)

• Machiavelli,
author (*The Prince*)

• Shakespeare, author
(*Romeo and Juliet, Hamlet*)

1450	1500	1550	1600

WORLD EVENTS

• Gutenberg invents printing press (*1454*)   • Martin Luther ignites Protestant Reformation (*1517*)

• Columbus travels to America (*1492*)

• Magellan circles globe (*1519*)

• Copernicus begins modern astronomy (*1543*)

• First European contact with Japan (*1549*)

35

THE BAROQUE ERA

MUSIC

Music and the arts (and even clothing) became fancier and more dramatic in the *Baroque* era (about 1600-1750). Like the fancy decorations of Baroque church architecture, melodies were often played with *grace notes*, or quick nearby tones added to decorate them. Rhythms became more complex with time signatures, bar lines and faster-moving melodic lines. Our now familiar major and minor scales formed the basis for harmony, and chords were standardized to what we often hear today.

The harpsichord became the most popular keyboard instrument, with players often *improvising* (making up) their parts using the composer's chords and bass line. Violin making reached new heights in Italy. Operas, ballets and small orchestras were beginning to take shape, as composers specified the exact instruments, tempos and dynamics to be performed.

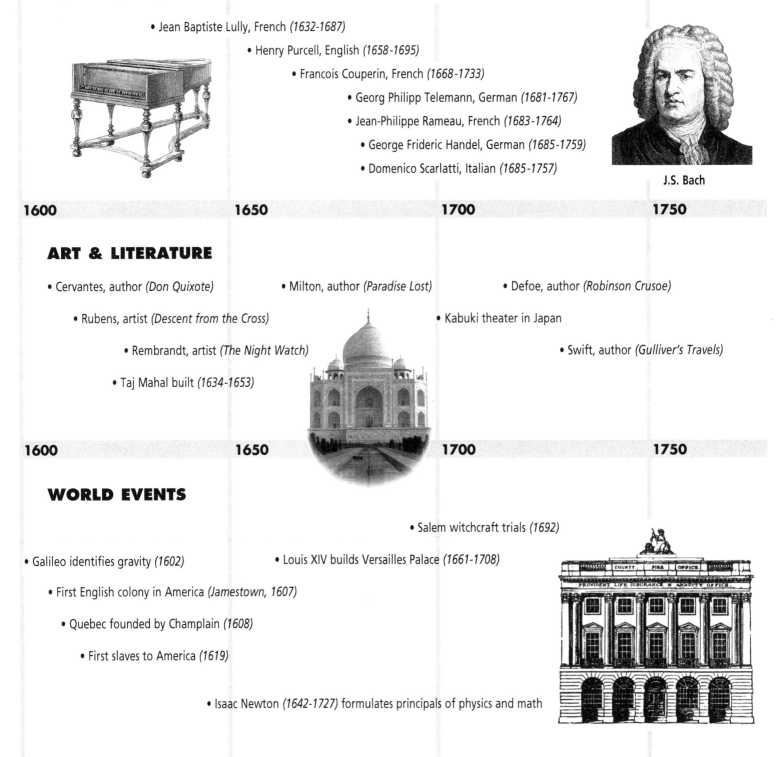

• Jean Baptiste Lully, French *(1632-1687)*

• Henry Purcell, English *(1658-1695)*

• Francois Couperin, French *(1668-1733)*

• Georg Philipp Telemann, German *(1681-1767)*

• Jean-Philippe Rameau, French *(1683-1764)*

• George Frideric Handel, German *(1685-1759)*

• Domenico Scarlatti, Italian *(1685-1757)*

J.S. Bach

ART & LITERATURE

• Cervantes, author *(Don Quixote)*

• Milton, author *(Paradise Lost)*

• Defoe, author *(Robinson Crusoe)*

• Rubens, artist *(Descent from the Cross)*

• Kabuki theater in Japan

• Rembrandt, artist *(The Night Watch)*

• Swift, author *(Gulliver's Travels)*

• Taj Mahal built *(1634-1653)*

WORLD EVENTS

• Salem witchcraft trials *(1692)*

• Galileo identifies gravity *(1602)*

• Louis XIV builds Versailles Palace *(1661-1708)*

• First English colony in America *(Jamestown, 1607)*

• Quebec founded by Champlain *(1608)*

• First slaves to America *(1619)*

• Isaac Newton *(1642-1727)* formulates principals of physics and math

THE CLASSICAL ERA

1750	1775	1800	1820

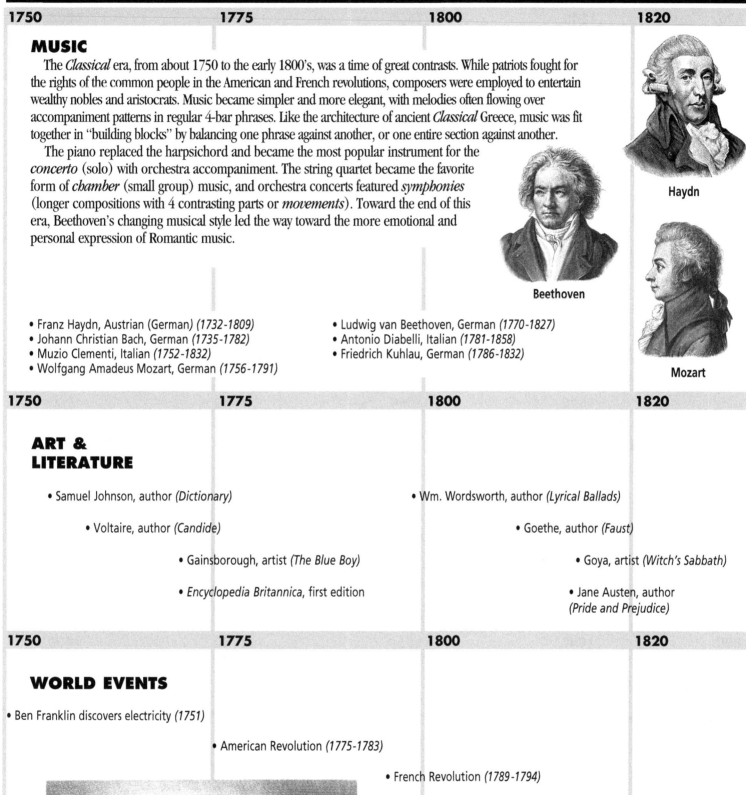

MUSIC

The *Classical* era, from about 1750 to the early 1800's, was a time of great contrasts. While patriots fought for the rights of the common people in the American and French revolutions, composers were employed to entertain wealthy nobles and aristocrats. Music became simpler and more elegant, with melodies often flowing over accompaniment patterns in regular 4-bar phrases. Like the architecture of ancient *Classical* Greece, music was fit together in "building blocks" by balancing one phrase against another, or one entire section against another.

The piano replaced the harpsichord and became the most popular instrument for the *concerto* (solo) with orchestra accompaniment. The string quartet became the favorite form of *chamber* (small group) music, and orchestra concerts featured *symphonies* (longer compositions with 4 contrasting parts or *movements*). Toward the end of this era, Beethoven's changing musical style led the way toward the more emotional and personal expression of Romantic music.

Haydn

Beethoven

Mozart

- Franz Haydn, Austrian (German) *(1732-1809)*
- Johann Christian Bach, German *(1735-1782)*
- Muzio Clementi, Italian *(1752-1832)*
- Wolfgang Amadeus Mozart, German *(1756-1791)*

- Ludwig van Beethoven, German *(1770-1827)*
- Antonio Diabelli, Italian *(1781-1858)*
- Friedrich Kuhlau, German *(1786-1832)*

1750	1775	1800	1820

ART & LITERATURE

- Samuel Johnson, author *(Dictionary)*

  - Voltaire, author *(Candide)*

    - Gainsborough, artist *(The Blue Boy)*

    - *Encyclopedia Britannica*, first edition

- Wm. Wordsworth, author *(Lyrical Ballads)*

  - Goethe, author *(Faust)*

    - Goya, artist *(Witch's Sabbath)*

    - Jane Austen, author *(Pride and Prejudice)*

1750	1775	1800	1820

WORLD EVENTS

- Ben Franklin discovers electricity *(1751)*

  - American Revolution *(1775-1783)*

    - French Revolution *(1789-1794)*

      - Napoleon crowned Emperor of France *(1804)*

      - Lewis and Clark explore northwest *(1804)*

        - Metronome invented *(1815)*

          - First steamship crosses Atlantic *(1819)*

THE ROMANTIC ERA

MUSIC

The last compositions of Beethoven were among the first of the new *Romantic* era, lasting from the early 1800's to about 1900. No longer employed by churches or nobles, composers became free from Classical restraints and expressed their personal emotions through their music. Instead of simple titles like *Concerto* or *Symphony*, they would often add descriptive titles like *Witches' Dance* or *To The New World*. Orchestras became larger, including nearly all the standard instruments we now use. Composers began to write much more difficult and complex music, featuring more "colorful" instrument combinations and harmonies.

Nationalism was an important trend in this era. Composers used folk music and folk legends (especially in Russia, eastern Europe and Scandinavia) to identify their music with their native lands. Today's concert audiences still generally prefer the drama of Romantic music to any other kind.

Schumann

Brahms

- Franz Schubert, German *(1797-1828)*
- Felix Mendelssohn, German *(1809-1847)*
- Friedrich Burgmuller, German *(1806-1874)*
- Frederic Francois Chopin, Polish *(1810-1849)*
- Robert Schumann, German *(1810-1856)*
- Franz Liszt, Hungarian *(1811-1886)*
- Stephen Heller, German *(1813-1888)*
- Fritz Spindler, German *(1817-1905)*

- Cornelius Gurlitt, German *(1820-1901)*
- Cesar Auguste Franck, French *(1822-1890)*
- Johannes Brahms, German *(1833-1897)*
- Camille Saint-Saens, French *(1835-1921)*
- Modest Mussorgsky, Russian *(1839-1881)*
- Peter Ilyich Tchaikovsky, Russian *(1840-1893)*
- Edvard Grieg, Norwegian *(1844-1908)*

ART & LITERATURE

- Charles Dickens, author *(The Pickwick Papers, David Copperfield)*

- Pierre Renoir, artist *(Luncheon of the Boating Party)*

- Harriet Beecher Stowe, author *(Uncle Tom's Cabin)*

- Lewis Carroll, author *(Alice In Wonderland)*

- Louisa May Alcott, author *(Little Women)*

- Jules Verne, author *(20,000 Leagues Under The Sea)*
- Claude Monet, artist *(Gare Saint-Lazare)*
- Mark Twain, author *(Tom Sawyer, Huckleberry Finn)*

- Vincent van Gogh, artist *(The Sunflowers)*

- Rudyard Kipling, author *(Jungle Book)*

WORLD EVENTS

- First railroad *(1830)*
- Samuel Morse invents telegraph *(1837)*
- First photography *(1838)*

- American Civil War *(1861-1865)*

- Alexander Graham Bell invents telephone *(1876)*

- Edison invents phonograph, practical light bulb, movie projector *(1877-1888)*

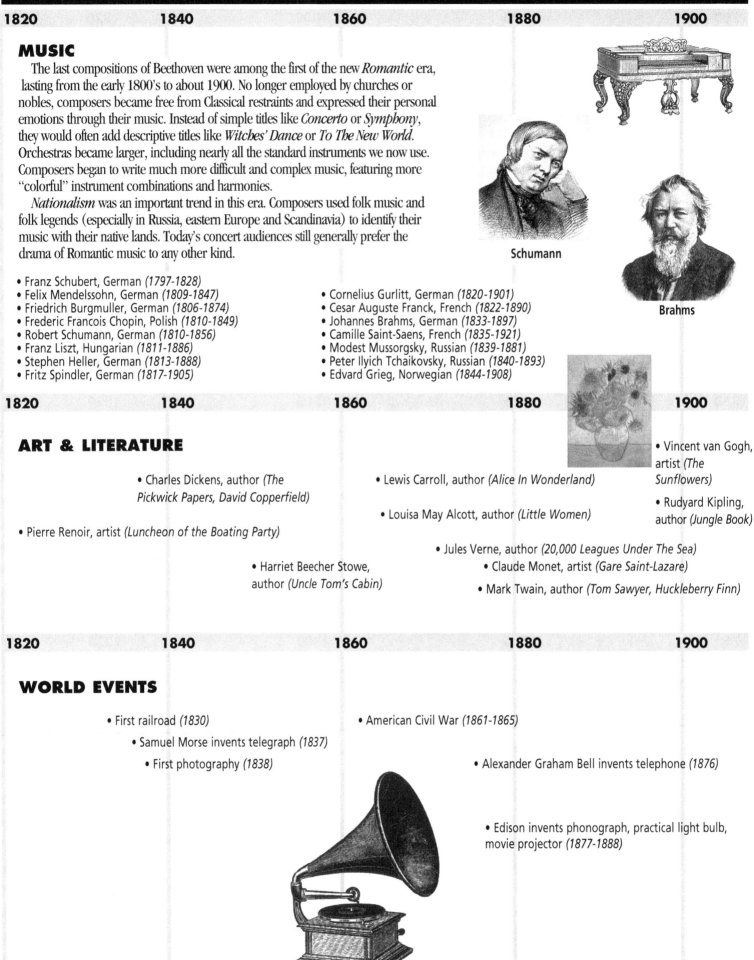

1900	1925	1950	1975	2000

- Edward MacDowell, American *(1861-1908)*
- Claude Debussy, French *(1862-1918)*
- Alexander Scriabin, Russian *(1872-1915)*
- Sergei Rachmaninoff, Russian *(1873-1943)*
- Arnold Schoenberg, German *(1874-1950)*
- Maurice Ravel, French *(1875-1937)*
- Bela Bartok, Hungarian *(1881-1945)*
- Heitor Villa-Lobos, Brazilian *(1881-1959)*
- Igor Stravinsky, Russian *(1882-1971)*
- Sergei Prokofieff, Russian *(1891-1952)*
- Paul Hindemith, German *(1895-1963)*
- George Gershwin, American *(1898-1937)*
- Aaron Copland, American *(1900-1990)*
- Aram Khachaturian, Russian *(1903-1978)*
- Dmitri Kabalevsky, Russian *(1904-1986)*
- Dmitri Shostakovich, Russian *(1906-1975)*
- Samuel Barber, American *(1910-1981)*
- Norman Dello Joio, American *(1913-   )*
- Vincent Persichetti, American *(1915-1987)*
- Philip Glass, American *(1937-   )*

MUSIC

The *20th century* was a diverse era of new ideas that "broke the rules" of traditional music. Styles of music moved in many different directions.

Impressionist composers Debussy and Ravel wrote music that seems more vague and blurred than the Romantics. New slightly-dissonant chords were used, and like Impressionist paintings, much of their music describes an impression of nature.

Composer Arnold Schoenberg devised a way to throw away all the old ideas of harmony by creating *12-tone* music. All 12 tones of the chromatic scale were used equally, with no single pitch forming a "key center."

Some of the music of Stravinsky and others was written in a *Neo-Classical* style (or "new" classical). This was a return to the Classical principals of balance and form, and to music that did *not* describe any scene or emotion.

Composers have experimented with many ideas: some music is based on the laws of chance, some is drawn on graph paper, some lets the performers decide when or what to play, and some is combined with electronic or other sounds.

Popular music like jazz, country, folk, and rock & roll has had a significant impact on 20th century life and has influenced great composers like Aaron Copland and Leonard Bernstein. And the new technology of computers and electronic instruments has had a major effect on the ways music is composed, performed and recorded.

1900	1925	1950	1975	2000

ART & LITERATURE

- Robert Frost, author *(Stopping by Woods on a Snowy Evening)*
- Pablo Picasso, artist *(Three Musicians)*
- J.R.R. Tolkien, author *(The Lord of the Rings)*
- F. Scott Fitzgerald, author *(The Great Gatsby)*
- Andy Warhol, artist *(Pop art)*
- Salvador Dali, artist *(Soft Watches)*
- Norman Mailer, author *(The Executioner's Song)*
- John Steinbeck, author *(The Grapes of Wrath)*
- Ernest Hemingway, author *(For Whom the Bell Tolls)*
- Andrew Wyeth, artist *(Christina's World)*
- George Orwell, author *(1984)*

1900	1925	1950	1975	2000

WORLD EVENTS

- First airplane flight *(1903)*
- Television invented *(1927)*
- Berlin Wall built *(1961)*
- Destruction of Berlin Wall *(1989)*
- World War I *(1914-1918)*
- World War II *(1939–1945)*
- John F. Kennedy assassinated *(1963)*
- First radio program *(1920)*
- Civil rights march in Alabama *(1965)*
- First satellite launched *(1957)*
- Man walks on the moon *(1969)*
- Vietnam War ends *(1975)*
- Personal computers *(1975)*

JOURNEY THROUGH THE CLASSICS

COMPILED AND EDITED BY JENNIFER LINN

Journey Through the Classics is a four-volume piano repertoire series designed to lead students seamlessly from the easiest classics to the intermediate masterworks. The graded pieces are presented in a progressive order and feature a variety of classical favorites essential to any piano student's educational foundation. The authentic repertoire is ideal for auditions and recitals and each book includes a handy reference chart with the key, composer, stylistic period, and challenge elements listed for each piece. Quality and value make this series a perfect classical companion for any method.

BOOK 1 ELEMENTARY
00296870 Book Only..........................$6.99
00142808 Book/Online Audio........$8.99

BOOK 2 LATE ELEMENTARY
00296871 Book Only..........................$6.99
00142809 Book/Online Audio........$8.99

BOOK 3 EARLY INTERMEDIATE
00296872 Book Only..........................$6.99
00142810 Book/Online Audio........$8.99

BOOK 4 INTERMEDIATE
00296873 Book Only..........................$7.99
00142811 Book/Online Audio........$9.99

JOURNEY THROUGH THE CLASSICS COMPLETE
(all 4 levels included in one book)
00110217 Book Only.......................$17.99
00123124 Book/Online Audio.....$24.99

HAL•LEONARD®

www.halleonard.com

Prices, contents, and availability subject to change without notice.